READ
...contemplate

HEED
...integrate

LEAD
... by example

READ
...contemplate

HEED
...integrate

LEAD
... by example

Dee Erica

© **Copyright 2020 Dee Erica Tze**

All rights reserved. Without limiting the rights under copyright reserved above, no part of this publication may be reproduced, stored in or introduced into a retrieval system, or transmitted, in any form or by any means (electronic, mechanical, photocopying, recording or otherwise), without the prior written permission of the copyright owner.

Disclaimer: The author does not provide medical advice or prescribe the use of any technique as a form of treatment for physical, emotional or medical problems without the advice of a physician, either directly or indirectly. The intent of the author is only to offer information to help you in your quest for spiritual and emotional wellbeing. In the event you use any of the information in this book for yourself, the author and the publisher assume no responsibility.

Publishing Details:

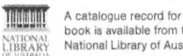
A catalogue record for this book is available from the National Library of Australia

ISBN: 978-0-6484500-3-0 (Paperback)
ISBN: 978-0-6484500-4-7 (Ebook)

Cover Design: Pickawoowoo Publishing Group, Laila Savolainen
Interior Layout: Pickawoowoo Publishing Group

Printing and channel distribution: Lightning Source / Ingram

Dedication

Dedicated to Luca Eli

You maybe young, too young to even read, I promise to leave you a world of peace and harmony, this book is my first step in achieving my promise, Lao Tze's words are timeless and will be waiting for you when you are ready to comprehend the meaning.

Whilst I am not always able to be with you in person, I am always with you in spirit my precious boy.

You will only have to pick up this book to know and understand how much I love you, sharing the first three months of your life is a memory I shall always treasure, singing you to sleep, our walks, hearing you say Mum for the first time. The kisses you blow to me on Facetime are priceless…may you always find peace in your heart, beauty in the world and remain true to yourself.

This book is a blueprint for living in harmony with all that is, I hope as you get older you read the verses and understand the importance of Lao Tze's wisdom and the importance of living from your heart not your head and always remain in a state of gratitude.

Our planet is in your hands, you are the future.

*A treasure doesn't have to be clad in gold for
all to see, it can and is, contained in thee*

My Granma Loves Me I know She Does

Introduction

The Tao Te Ching for Contemplation and Integration

The Tao Te Ching was written well over 2,500 years ago, words Lao Tze wrote for that time period, yet words which are even more relevant for today, tomorrow and whilst ever there is life on planet Earth. The verses were a vision of peace and harmony from an author disillusioned with life as it unfolded before him, he wrote the 81 verses before leaving and becoming a recluse. History reports him as not being sighted again.

Lao Tze is purported to be the greatest philosopher who ever walked on Earth, after you read his words, you too will understand how history derived this conclusion.

The Tao is a spiritual way of being, it is not a religion, it is purely a way of life to which we all should aspire as a means of living in harmony.

The 81 verses covers many topics, to name a few:

- Act but not compete
- Appreciating our five senses

- Be an individual
- Be content with what you have
- Be fair not harsh
- Be in balance
- Be open to what you don't know
- Cause no harm
- Calm
- Death
- Deceit
- Duality
- Ego
- Equality
- Flexibility
- Humility
- Impartiality
- Loving ourselves
- Meditation
- Not to abuse power
- Plan ahead and come from love
- Resentment
- Respect
- Silence is golden
- Treat others as you wish to be treated
- Violence

Ancient Wisdom, modern twist, add a dash of intelligence
The 'Old Master' gave us a way, to live our life everyday
Be the Captain of your own ship
Steer your course by the guiding light
Lead by example

And be like Lao Tze
In everything you say and do
A lighthouse does but stand and shine
And be a beacon, so others may

In their own sweet time, Find the Way

It is imperative if we are to survive and move forward into the 5th Dimension we need to be living in accordance with the Tao, living in a world devoid of judgment, violence, disrespect, living as one in love and harmony, respectful of Mother Earth and our fellow man, regardless of colour or race.

Pollution and chemicals must be lessened or abolished completely as we live in harmony with our fellow man, animals, plants and the crystal and mineral kingdom. Mining isn't condoned unless it serves the Greater Good of all and undertaken in accordance with the wishes of Mother Earth. Mother Earth is rebelling now against humanities treatment of her, she is undergoing a transition or rebirth which must occur however, she requires our assistance in order to undo all the harm we have done to her for thousands of years.

Many versions have been translated since the infamous 81 verses were written. I have it from a reliable source that none of the many versions are entirely correct. There are some who question, if in fact, Lao Tze existed at all.

How could the versions be correct, no one has been in contact with the author to verify the translations? Until now! They were voiced and written in an ancient language, one which in itself is difficult to translate even under optimal circumstances. Much has been lost with the various translations. It is what it is. Those who tried to translate these important verses did their best to fulfil the task at hand, unfortunately they fall a little short of the mark and the time has come to correct the situation.

Lao Tze introduced himself to me when I began to channel in March 2009, he is a delightful soul whom I have come to love in this life as well as the life I had known previously. I received advice from a medium that the spirit I was channeling was Lao 'something' as she was unable to interpret his last name. At the time (in this life) I had absolutely no idea who he was/had been, so it was time for research. Apart from knowing he was from ancient China and his first name was Lao, I was in the dark so I decided to ask the question. I put pen to paper and asked him his name, my hand began to write LAO TZE in block letters, without any assistance from me. Unreal! I asked how he pronounced his name and his advice was…sounds like towel. The jury remains out on as to how to pronounce TZE it seems different depending upon whom you ask.

As with the translation of the verses, Lao Tze's name was also open for translation and has many different versions of Lao Tze, Lao Tse, Lao Tsu Laozi. TZE is the version I received so I work with that. I do know that prior to learning his correct name all I knew was that I was channeling someone with whom I was very familiar and had a strong affinity, the ease with which we spoke allowed me to assume we knew each other very well (previously from another time and place).

Lao Tze has not incarnated on Earth since his incarnation as Lao Tze, he feels the time is right for his words to be rewritten as he intended them, only this time written in a way and a language we can understand and interpret without pondering what he may have meant. For whatever reason Lao Tze has not channeled previously to anyone, I can only assume the reason for this will be revealed, as in all things...in Divine time.

In my first book, 'I Make Mark' I outlined the Holistic Wheel Theory which was channeled to me with instructions that it was to be included at the end of that particular book. I have included it in this book as a means of reference as to where and how the Holistic Wheel Theory fits into the life Lao Tze envisaged when he wrote the Tao Te Ching. In Verse 11, Lao Tze speaks of thirty spokes so I am assuming this is the desired amount for which we aim whilst designing our own personal Wheel.

Wayne Dyer's book 'Living the Wisdom of the Tao' was really my only reference point for many years, as I had had difficulty trying to interpret any of the translated versions. I was amazed and in awe of the person who gave this wisdom to the world, how could I not be? If we were to live in accordance with the Tao, we wouldn't need Governments, Police, Prisons, we would self regulate and intuitively and instinctively respect everything and everyone with whom we make contact.

Imagine a world where we lived in community villages where everyone helped everyone without conflict – well we can achieve this state simply by following the teachings of this wonderful man.

Lao Tze outlines a blueprint for good governance and how this has the potential to achieve an effective, harmonious yet respected head of state. To lead always with humility, honesty, compassion and respect, and, in doing so, apply the same qualities to our own behaviour amid the activities of our daily life.

Why I have been chosen for this amazing, humbling experience? As I sit and write, I do not have an answer for you, I only know it is an honour and a privilege to undertake and channel the current day version of these infamous verses. An honour to work with a beautiful soul, who is my Spiritual father, a Master, a mentor, my guiding light and indeed an amazing friend who at times has me in stitches laughing at his jokes, other times scolding me as any father would. He isn't someone who puts himself on a pedestal and demands we listen and heed his words. Lao Tze is a humble man, with a flowing white beard who holds the wisdom of the world on our behalf and wishes only to share his philosophy with us, in the quest for a better earth and for us to attain a higher level of consciousness.

A book will be channeled by Lao Tze at a later date, one which explains in more detail the full meaning of each verse, a workbook if you like with examples, leaving the reader in no doubt as to the message the author is endeavoring to convey.

In 'I Make Mark' I state that after reading Wayne Dyer's book I deduced that one does not have to know the Tao to be living the Tao, we incorporate it into our daily lives without even realizing it. When you read the verses you will understand what I mean by this statement. Living in accordance with the Tao will make your life and those of the people around you a truly wonderful experience. An experience Lao Tze wishes for all, it is his gift of peace and harmony to humanity.

I ask you to read his words, absorb, integrate and undertake, should this not be possible then please, at least read with an open mind and contemplate the meaning of each verse. My hope is for some, if not all the verses, to speak to you and reach your heart.

Lao Tze in many instances, refers to living and coming from the heart space, he refers to it as returning to one's roots. When we are born, we know only love and it is within our capacity to remain in this state. It isn't always that simple, but it can be if we consciously incorporate the wisdom of the Tao into our daily lives.

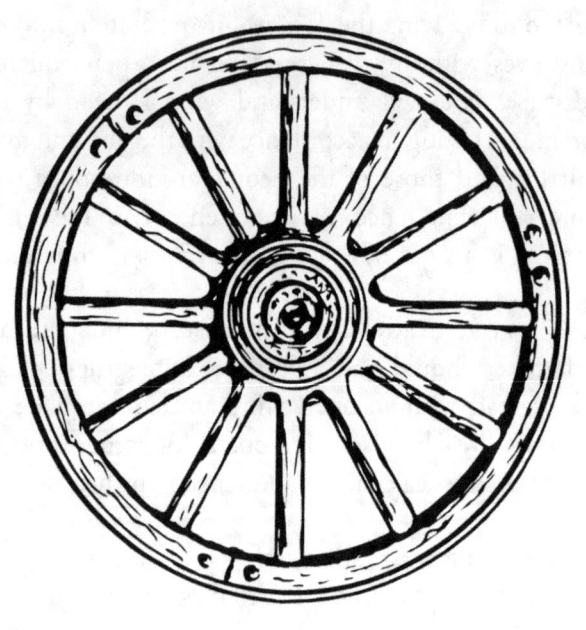

The Holistic Wheel Theory

Balance is the key to most things in life.

Imagine if you will, ***a wheel***, like you would see on a wagon from days of old. It has 3 major components.

The ***outer rim*** is the ***framework*** which holds everything together.

The ***centre or hub*** – the ***pivotal point***.

The ***individual spokes***.

Living the Tao is the **fundamental framework** for living as one, working as one, moving forward as one. Without a sturdy framework the wheel cannot function.

The ***centre*** or ***pivotal point*** is ***spirituality*** and your role in the Divine Plan. I am not speaking religion I am speaking spiritual awareness.

The ***spokes*** are another mandatory element of the wheel. If the spokes are not balanced moving forward will not be smooth.

The spokes include but are not limited to: Self love, Chemical Free, Whole Foods, Exercise, Dental Care, Rest, Relaxation Stress Free, Happiness, Love, Compassion, Respect, Forgiveness, Honesty, Medical Care with respect to Holistic Therapies and values, Counselling, Meditation, Vitamin and Supplements, Respect for Mother Earth.

Refer completed version contained in 'I MAKE MARK'… should you require further insight…build your wheel in accordance with your intuition, your inner knowing, you are the only one who knows what is best for you…

With this in mind I shall begin to channel the 81 verses of the Tao Te Ching as Lao Tze intended them and pray I channel them with accuracy and with the respect they so deserve.

Verse One

Source is not one that can be
named, seen nor touched
Source is infinite
Source is eternal
Source is spiritual not religious
Source created Heaven and Earth
Source created all creatures great and small
Source does not believe in power or control at all
Tao cannot be quantified
Tao is Source
Tao and Source are one and same
Live the Tao and you shall see
How clear, everything can be
Live the Tao and you are living as Source intended
Live the Tao and the mysteries of
the Universe will unfold

*To Live the Tao as Source intended, is to
know that all has transcended, for we shall
always be, privy to all for eternity*

Verse Two

Duality creates beautiful and ugly, good and evil
Something and nothing are products of the same
Difficult and easy compliment each other
The long and the short, the high and the low
Note and sound harmonise to
produce music for our souls
The sage takes no action and practices teaching
But he does not speak, he sees no need
Duality is day and night
Life is given, yet free will is expected
Without duality there would be no free will
We are given what we require
Yet not expected to give in return
Tao accomplishes its tasks yet claims
no acknowledgement
It is because it lays no claim that
acknowledgement prevails

Duality is important for us to note, without duality, we would have no frame of reference, free will is assured, requirements are met, without expectation or any regret

Verse Three

No action creates order

Not to place importance on valuables
gives them immunity against theft

Treat all men as equal and they will come to no harm

Not to flaunt that which is desirable causes no envy

Do that which consists of taking no
action, and order will prevail

To flaunt, to boast and to idolize

Is to create a desire for which some aspire

By foul or fair, they do not care

Taking no action is to tone it down

And very humbly wear your crown

Be content with all you that you have

For happiness lies in your heart, not your head

*Take no action and you will see,
profound protection and harmony*

Verse Four

The Way, the path is there for all of us
Our wheels move along old ruts
Many have gone before us
Yet the path does not wear
It is the path of our ancestors
We leave no footprints on this path
It is as if we were not even there
Yet it takes us Home

The Way Home, though not visible, is there for us,
so we can find, eternal grace on the other side

Verse Five

Silence is golden

Likened to the space between Heaven and Earth

We are not forgotten on Earth

We are watched over to exercise our free will

Source is there when we ask

Source is there when we pray

Yet Source will not intervene unless requested to do so

Source is vast yet seemingly empty at the same time

Source will respond, yet silence with prevail

Silence carries information from Source

Silence your mind and you too will hear

Silence is golden, when you do pray, a response will be given and sent your way

Verse Six

The Way lies dormant but never dies
The gateway to the mysterious
Is there when required
It takes but a moment
To open your heart
Close your eyes
The third eye opens…..
Allow the light
To enter thru your heart
Past, present and future will then be revealed

*The gifts are there for all to be, awakened
and knowing for eternity*

Verse Seven

Heaven and Earth have no ego
Source has no ego yet remains revered
The sage puts himself last, yet comes first
Serve without ego and your tasks will be accomplished
Open your heart and get out of your head
You find love in your heart
Fear in your head
Devoid of ego
Love overrides fear
Fear has nowhere to go
There is only fear or love
Fear you will not find, in Heaven above
So whilst on Earth
Always remember
To live from your heart
For tis the place to come from love

Ego has no place to be, residing in thee or humanity, come from love, be of love, for this is the message I send from above

Verse Eight

Acting in accordance with the highest good of all
Can be likened to water
Water benefits many and much,
yet does not try to rule
In a home it is the love that matters
In quality of mind it is depth that matters
In a friend it is loyalty that matters
In speech it is sincerity that matters
In government it is order and fairness that matters
In business it is the ability that matters
In action it is timeliness that matters
So be like the water, flow without the need to control
Touch yet do not change
These actions are in accordance with the
Highest good of all

*Be like water and you shall flow,
without the need to feel control*

Verse Nine

Humility
To be humble is a virtue
To be humble is being true to who you are
Humility is afforded respect
For those who have it will be lauded by all
But lose humility and you will lose it all
To succeed without the need for acknowledgement
Is the way of Heaven

To be humble is a virtue, lose humility
and you shall lose it all

Verse Ten

Upon death, our bodies return to the Earth
Our soul ascends to Heaven
The invisible gateway allows us thru
so we may come to Earth
It allows us thru so we may return Home
Taking no action and allowing
Claiming no possessions
Exacting no gratitude
Exercising no authority
Such is called the mysterious virtue

The mysterious virtue is for one and all, surrender is the key and forget what you know, for this is simply the way things go

Verse Eleven

The wheel may have thirty spokes
Yet it shares but one hub
The hub is but an empty space
Yet it moves the cart
A vessel is empty
Yet it is the empty space we need
Cut out doors and windows to make a room
Yet it is the empty space which makes the room
Thus what we gain is Something,
Yet it is by virtue of Nothing
That this can be put to use

An empty space, is an open mind, where
nothing is something for you to find

Verse Twelve

We have five senses
Yet we strive for much more to give us excitement
Too many goods can impede our progress
To fill our heart with love
Will provide deep fulfillment
Possessions cannot fill this void
Therefore the sage discards one and takes the other

*Be like the Sage and be content, for
our five senses are Heaven sent*

Verse Thirteen

Compliments and criticism can both cause discomfort
Body image worries us
Those who treat their bodies with respect
Will in turn gain respect
Those who love their bodies
Will in turn gain love
We can't love others unless we first love ourselves
He who values his body more than power
Can be entrusted with the nation
He who values his body over the nation
Can be entrusted custody of the nation
We have but one body
Cherish, honour and respect it
And it will serve well
To receive love you must first love yourself

We are given one body, to love and respect, loves begins in this space, so without any disgrace, first loving yourself is the golden rule

Verse Fourteen

We come from nothing
We return to nothing
Yet nothing is something
It cannot be seen
It cannot be heard
It cannot be touched
This is called the shape that has no shape
The image that is without substance
You will not see its head
Nor it rear
Hold fast to these thoughts of our origin
For they help us understand the realm of today
The ability to know the beginning
Is called the thread running through the Way

*From this space of nothingness it opens
us up, to understand everything*

Verse Fifteen

Those who knew and understood Tao
Knew the Way
Were seen as subtle, mysterious, profound
Too profound to be known
It is because he could not be known
That the description is vague
He was elusive, tentative, hesitant
He who believes in the Way
Slowly comes to life
And is fulfilled and nourished

To believe in the Way, is to know Home, to believe in the Way, is to know Source, to know Source is to know peace and contentment

Verse Sixteen

I do my utmost to attain emptiness
I hold firmly to stillness
All creatures return to their separate roots
Returning to one's roots is known as stillness
This is what is meant by returning to one's destiny
Returning to one's destiny is known as the constant
Knowledge of the constant is known as discernment
One should act only from knowledge of the constant
This brings impartiality
Remain an individual
Impartiality leads to enlightenment
Enlightenment to Heaven
Heaven is the Way
The Way to eternal life
To live in this accord
Affords a life of peace and calm

No harm befalls the owner of calm
Emptiness is a place to be, stillness is returning to one's destiny, for here we are able to be, impartial and know eternity

Verse Seventeen

The most proficient of rulers is but a
shadowy presence to his subjects

There are many types of rulers

The ruler they love and praise

The ruler they fear

The ruler with whom they take liberties

When there is insufficient faith,
there is lack of good faith

The wise ruler does not utter words lightly

He leads by example

When his task is accomplished and his work is done

The people all say: "It happened to us naturally"

Lead by Example

for

*Where there is insufficient faith,
there is a lack of good faith*

Verse Eighteen

When we no longer follow the Way
Dissention follows
We become critical of those with talent
Hypocrisy is rife
When our family members and are at odds
The children follow this behaviour
When the state is in chaos and darkness
Many too will follow this path

*Follow the Way, for a happier life, for in
this state there will be way less strife*

Verse Nineteen

If we do not listen and heed the words of the sage
If we do not listen to the words of the wise
If we discard good, charitable and our morals
Again others will follow
If we embrace that which is constant
Undertake our work without profit
We discard the need for others to covet
The people must have something to
which they can align themselves
Exhibit the unadorned and embrace
the uncarved block
Discard ego and have few desires as possible
Embrace that which is constant
Be a role model for those who require guidance
Lead by example

*Heed the words of the sage and the wise, follow
the Way, in doing so embrace and be content,
knowing as a role model, you do present*

Verse Twenty

The gap between yes and no
The gap between good and evil
The distance between rich and poor
How great is this distance?
Does it vary for each of us?
Must we fear what others fear?
The masses are joyous, ignorant
I feel like I am lacking, wanting
The masses have more than enough
Yet still I feel listless
I alone seem to be in want
Some people are certain
My mind seems blank
Some people are alert
I alone am drowsy
I am confused
Yet calm like the sea

Like a high wind that never ceases
The masses appear to all have a purpose
I am different from others and value my connection to source

It is ok to be an individual just like me

Verse Twenty One

A man of great virtue
Follows the Way and only the Way
As a thing the Way is
Shadowy, indistinct
Yet it has substance within
An essence
The essence is genuine
Essence dates back to the beginning
Essence is Source
Source is our beginning
We can connect with our fathers
Like our fathers did before us
We are the same
We are ONE

Follow the Way and you will see, We are the same, We are, but One

Verse Twenty Two

Bowed down then preserved
Bent then straight
Hollow then full
Worn then new
Some understand
Some do not
The sage embraces the One and is a model for all
He does not show himself, and so is conspicuous
He does not consider himself
right, and so is illustrious
He does not brag, and so has merit
He does not boast, and so endures
It is because he does not compete that
no one competes with him
The ancient saying "Bowed down then
preserved" is no empty saying
Truly if one is bowed down one is
able to endure until the end

To be bowed down and flexible is to endure
Act but not compete, is the golden rule of which I speak

Verse Twenty Three

To speak rarely
Is to be natural
A gusty wind cannot last, a sudden downpour cannot last
Heaven and earth produce these states
If these states are unable to go on for long periods
Much less can man
This is why one follows the Way
A man of the Way conforms to the Way
A man of virtue conforms to virtue
He who conforms to the Way is gladly accepted by the Way
He who conforms to virtue is gladly accepted by virtue
He who chooses not to follow the Way is accepted by this state
When faith and guidance are lacking, lack of good faith follows

*When faith and guidance are lacking,
lack of good faith follows*

Verse Twenty Four

Follow the Way and life is in balance
We do not need to be seen
We do not need to brag
We do not need to boast
The Way has no need for such displays
And he who follows the Way has no need for them

He who follows the Way is in balance

Verse Twenty Five

I call it 'The Way'
There is confusion as to how it was formed
Born before Heaven and Earth
Silent and seemingly empty
It stands alone and does not change
Goes round and does not weary
It is capable of being the mother of the world
I call it 'the great'
It is far away yet near
Hence the Way is great, Heaven is great, Earth is great
The creator of all that is, is great
Man models himself on earth,
Earth on Heaven
Heaven on the Way
This is the natural order

There is no better model to which to aspire,
silent and seemingly empty, far yet near,
as it is in Heaven, so it is here

Verse Twenty Six

To remain calm and serene when turmoil abounds
Is an art form to which all should aspire
Do not wait until in the safety of your own home
To allow calm and serene to prevail and rest again
Take it with you whilst travelling all day
Leaders hear my plea, lead by example
For all to see
Apportioning blame to others for
the state of your mind
Will not bring you to the state of being you seek
You alone own your feelings and actions
Empty your mind of judgements
Allowing yourself to be blown to and fro
Means you have lost touch with your roots
To be restless is a loss of self-mastery
Reclaim the calm, reclaim your inner power

To reclaim your calm, is to reclaim your inner power
Apportioning blame to others for the state of your mind, will not bring you to the state of peace you seek

Verse Twenty Seven

Travel through life with your inner
knowing, your inner light
For you are the Truth
Travel without leaving a trace
Speak without causing harm
Give without keeping count
One who excels in tying uses no cords, yet
what he has tied cannot be undone
The Sage excels in saving people, so abandons no one
The Sage excels in saving things, so abandons nothing
The Sage is a teacher from whom students learn
The Sage learns what he needs to
teach from his students
Neither is more important
This is called the **essential**
Giving and receiving are one
This is called the **essential** and the **secret**

*To know the essential and the secret
is the Path of Illumination*

Verse Twenty Eight

Know the male

But keep to the role of the female

Balance the male/female within

Know the dark

But keep the light

Know honour

But keep to the role of the disgraced

Live virtuously with love, kindness and with the beauty with which you arrived

Live as Source intended by these preserving 'original qualities'

Be a role model

Be one with nature or the Way

Allow the Tao to guide you

Allow the river of life to flow through you

*To be in Balance is the message I give,
for me, it is, the only way to live*

Verse Twenty Nine

Source cannot be changed
It is sacred
Some lead, some follow
Some breathe gently, some breathe hard
Some are strong, some are weak
Some destroy; some are destroyed
The Sage avoids excess, extravagance and arrogance

The way of the sage is to act but not compete

Verse Thirty

Assist the Ruler by showing the Way
Where troops have camped
Brambles will grow
Where a mighty army has existed
Bad harvests will follow
A good Ruler does not intimidate, brag nor boast
A good Ruler shows no arrogance
Do no harm to fellow man
To do otherwise is going against the Way
That which goes against the Way
Comes to an early end

There is no future in being harsh, to think there is, is purely a farce, for more is attained through fair than foul, in achieving this, you will be living the Tao

Verse Thirty One

Artillery against man are ill omens
Those who follow the way
Have no use for such weapons
If compelled to use them do so with humility
There is no glory in victory
To glorify is to condone the killing of man
One who enjoys the killing of man
will not know Source
Mourn the loss of man
Weep over them with sorrow
When victorious in war
Observe the rules of mourning

Violence even well intentioned, always rebounds upon oneself, he who conquers is strong, but he who conquers himself is surely mighty, remember the fallen, as it should be, remember with grace and humility

Verse Thirty Two

The Way is nameless
No one can claim it
It is somewhere we attain to find
All do so, in our own sweet time
When we all achieve this state
Heaven and Earth will both rejoice
All will be equal for you and me
Forever in eternity
For we flow to the Way
As rivers to the sea
And that is how
It was meant to be

We flow to the Way, as rivers to the sea, for all shall be equal for you and me, forever in eternity
Equity in unity

Verse Thirty Three

Knowing others is wisdom
Knowing yourself is discernment
Overcoming others shows force
Overcoming yourself shows strength
He who knows contentment is rich
He who perseveres is a man of purpose
He who can maintain a course
Of knowing himself shall have a long life

When I let go of what I am, I become what I might be
Knowing others is wisdom, knowing
yourself is enlightenment

Verse Thirty Four

The Way is vast
Many rely on it for life
Yet it claims no authority
It accomplishes, yet does not brag
It clothes and feeds all
Yet does not claim to be their Master
It is because it never claims to be great
That is succeeds in being great

Be the chief but never the Lord, for in doing so, you shall reap your reward

Verse Thirty Five

Hold the image of Source with you
For it is with you in all that you do
You will come to no harm, be safe and sound
Music and food shall abound
It cannot be seen
It cannot be heard
But never a truer word have you heard
Hold the image of Source with you
Let it be shown, in all that you do

By holding the image of Source so dear, let it be clear for all to hear, peace, love, grace and humility, shall endure for you, for eternity

Verse Thirty Six

For it to shrink, it must first be whole
For it to stretch if must first hold fast
For it to be weak, it must first be strong
For it to be laid aside, it must first be set up
If you would take from something,
  you must first give to it
This is called subtle discernment
Balance is to know extremes
When to advance
When to retreat
For a balanced mind
Is a place of retreat

If you would take, you must first give, this is discernment

Verse Thirty Seven

The Way never acts, yet nothing is left undone
If our Rulers held fast to the Way
All of the nation would be transformed
If desires again tried to overtake,
they would be dismissed
For freedom from desire
Is something to which, we should all aspire
For if this should prevail, world peace would avail

*Freedom from desire, is something to
which we all should aspire*

Verse Thirty Eight

People often fail in the handling of affairs
when they are about to succeed
If one remains as careful at the end
as he was at the beginning
There will be no failure
For it is in the heart
And in the deed
Comes the means to succeed
But should you forget
Whence came the seed
And if the ending is based on greed
Failure will be inevitable

In the heart and in the deed, lies the secret to succeed

Verse Thirty Nine

The leaders on Earth hold a huge responsibility
For humans, flora and fauna
All are reliant on their good grace
In order to hold their vital place
We could all fall, like a stone
If those in charge, abuse their throne
If they were all, to follow the Way
We would all be safe, for another day
For us all to be as one
We need our leaders to be like the son
And follow the path of the chosen one

We could all fall like a stone, if those in power abuse their throne

Verse Forty

We are born from something and
something from nothing
Turning back is how the way moves
Weakness is the means to greatness

*We come from source, we return to source, surrender
is not a sign of weakness, it is allowing*

Verse Forty One

The Way is viewed in different lights
Viewed by many from different heights
Revered, feared and even jeered
One constant for all
Although it may not have any form
It is what it is
And those who know
Follow with grace
For they understand
Its vital place
To receive and accomplish
To know our place
Is all in the keeping
of our faith

To follow the Way, is to lead with good grace, for those who follow shall surely know, what it is like to succeed and receive

Verse Forty Two

One becomes many
Yet many become one
Yin and Yang are but part of the whole
We are alone
Yet we are not
This becomes a struggle for some
The violent will not come to a natural end

If this becomes a struggle for you, always remember you are part of the one and not the few

Verse Forty Three

The most submissive thing in the world
Can ride roughshod over the hardest in the world
Resorting to no action has great benefit
Teaching that uses no words
Is considered taking no action
The benefits of which but few understand

*Take no action and you shall find, a greater
understanding for all mankind*

Verse Forty Four

Your name or your person?
Your person or your goods?
Gain or loss?
Which is worth more?
To have too much is to know loss
Know contentment
And you will meet with no danger
You can endure

It takes not riches, nor fame nor greed, in order for you to endure and succeed

Verse Forty Five

Perfection and great fullness
Cannot be worn out nor drained
Restlessness overcomes cold
Stillness overcomes heat
By being quiet and still
One can be a leader

*Be a leader with calm and still for
this is the way to better fulfil*

Verse Forty Six

When the Way prevails
War is no longer required
There is no greater crime
Than having too many desires
There is no disaster than not being content
There is no greater misfortune than greed
Hence in being content
One has enough

There is no greater crime than having too many desires
Don't live in a state of discontent, with
all that you have, be content

Verse Forty Seven

Without going overseas
One can know the whole world
Without looking out the window
One can see the Way to heaven
The further one goes
The less one knows
The sage knows
The sage identifies without having to see
Accomplishes without having to act
Listen to your heart
And you shall be
Residing and living in harmony
For intuition was given to us
As a gift in which
To place our trust

The more I know, the more I realise I don't know
Listen to your heart, and you shall be,
residing and living in harmony

Verse Forty Eight

In the pursuit of learning, one knows more each day
In the pursuit of the Way, one does less each day
By doing nothing you achieve everything
And nothing is undone
By allowing you have won

*Surrender and you shall find, everything
will eventually, work out just fine*

Verse Forty Nine

The sage treats everyone the same
From doing so he gains
Goodness, good faith and grace
Though not all will understand
It is an unwritten law
Of the land

Do unto others as you would have them
do unto you, for then goodness, good faith
and grace shall also befall, unto you

Verse Fifty

Life and Death
If you choose life you will die
If you choose death you shall live
To value life is to have no fear
For neither man nor beast
Can harm you here
So keep the faith and you will see
There is no death for you and me
Tis only our body which does give in
For our soul continues to always be
Forever in eternity

*Death holds no fear when you believe
our soul continues on from here*

Verse Fifty One

The Way gives life
Virtue rears you like a Mother
Challenges gives you maturity
All revere the Way
And honour virtue
Yet neither claim possession
Nor expect gratitude
It exercises no authority
Such is called the mysterious virtue

Have respect for all, honour your journey and you shall find, a deep respect grows inside

A challenge is nothing for you to fear, it is but a lesson, for you to hear, if you wish to learn and to grow, be open to what you don't know

Verse Fifty Two

To see the small is called discernment
To hold fast to submissive is called strength
Use the light
But give up discernment
And misfortune may follow
This is known as following the constant

You do not have to show strength to be strong, you do not have to have much to be respected, by remaining humble you shall find you are leading the way for all mankind

Verse Fifty Three

If you follow the Way
And do not stray
A better land
Would be more at hand
For corruption would go
Crops would flourish
Hunger would no longer be
A problem for neither you nor me
No rich nor poor
No robbery
For all deserve equality

If we were all to follow the Way we will no longer be, sadly deprived of equality

Verse Fifty Four

The Way is a foundation
It drives not only you and me
But also our great nation
If we can get it right in our own self
It follows to the family
From the family it does move forth
Our into our community
From the community it does move forth
Out into the state itself
From the state it does move forth
Out into this world
We call Earth

It starts with one and then its two,
momentum begins with me and you

Verse Fifty Five

To possess virtue is to be pure
To know harmony is called the constant
To know the constant is called discernment

Live your life in perfect harmony, with the animals, plants, the birds and the bees, for it is only by following the Way, we gain strength, and know tranquility and longevity

Verse Fifty Six

One who knows does not speak
One who speaks does not know
Follow the way of our ancestors
This is known as the mysterious sameness
You cannot get close to it
You cannot touch it
You cannot bestow benefit on it
Nor can you do it harm
Yet the Way is valued by all who know

*Follow the Way and you will be,
lighting the path for others to see*

Verse Fifty Seven

Govern the country honestly
With lots of care and humility
Be respectful be humane
From this there will be
Much to gain
For the more rules you make
There are more to break
The more possessions you have
There is more to take
So keep it simple
And you shall see
Transformation will happen
Naturally

*Keep it simple and you shall see,
transformation happens naturally*

Verse Fifty Eight

The government lead the way
Whether good or bad
In every way
For if disharmony prevails
For all to see
It creates chaos
In everyone, every day
In every way
If the government lead by following the Way
We would all benefit
In every way

One does not have to shine to dazzle, follow the Way and shine your light, for no one could ask for a better sight

Verse Fifty Nine

A government rules best
When following the Way
For then it does less
But gains the most
Nothing cannot be overcome
There are no limits
By spreading deep roots
We all shall endure

*By holding firm to beliefs tried and true we
gain the strength to get us through*

Verse Sixty

Governing is best, if done with intent
Causing no harm
No major upset
For then the people with learn
To trust and respect
If you rule with no harm
You too shall learn
No harm is likely
to come to you
Much more can then be achieved
By a government
Intent on leading the Way

Lead the Way by causing no harm, no major upset, for this is how you earn respect

Verse Sixty One

The Way is to the World
As a river to a stream
One is great
The other small
Yet neither can exist
Without the other
Union of both
Is the key
For then both have found their proper place

Neither small nor large have more importance,
to unite the two, to be as one, provides
a better space to get things done

Verse Sixty Two

The Way offers hope for many to see
For in the faith holds a sanctuary
For it is many a good deed that shall win the day
Lead by example
And follow the Way
It holds far more value than a pot of gold
The Way has been revered
From days of old

*If you follow the Way, like in days of old,
you too will find, your pot of gold*

Verse Sixty Three

Do that which consists of taking no action
We can make things difficult when we try too hard
Make the small big and the few many
Many beginnings begin with small
Many difficulties begin with easy
The sage never attempts to be great
Which is why he is deemed great
If you plan ahead and come from love
You have the blessing of above

If you plan ahead and come from love,
respect your fellow man, easy is as easy does,
from which all things will be revered

Verse Sixty Four

Don't let resentment ever take hold
It is always best to speak your mind
For even a tree grows from a seed
And this it does in your mind
If at first you wish to succeed
Always remember this very creed
A journey of a thousand miles
Always begins with but one single step
If you always continue
With a true intent
The end result will be as you meant
But should you continue
Without this in mind
And lose sight of the value you had at the time
Failure you are more likely to find

Always finish as you began, come from love with true intent, and with the end you will be content
A journey of a thousand miles begins with one single step

Verse Sixty Five

There are two ways a government can choose to rule
If at first you choose to deceive
You may get more than you wish to receive
But if at first you choose goodwill
You shall surely remain in power still
To know which way in which to rule
Is known as the mysterious virtue
Mysterious virtue is profound and better by far
For in this state, peace will reign
With law and order to remain

*If you choose to deceive you may get more
than you wish to receive, if you always choose
goodwill, you will remain in your power still*

Verse Sixty Six

To be humble and take the lower road
To lead from behind is a state of mind
For if you want another to follow
It is best you show you too can be
Retained in your own humility
Loyalty will come your way
Hence have no need for hostility

*Retained in your own humility,
causes no need for hostility*

Verse Sixty Seven

The Way is vast and yet resembles nothing
There are three treasures to hold and cherish
Compassion, frugality and humility
In being compassionate one can be courageous
In being frugal one can expand
In not being a leader one can lead
But to forsake the former for the latter
Is a recipe for you to scatter
It shall not end well if you choose to be
Deficient in compassion and humility

*It shall not end well if you choose to be
deficient in compassion and humility*

Verse Sixty Eight

You can be a warrior without need to defeat
Be a fighter without the anger to meet
You can defeat the enemy by remaining calm
Humility is a real cool charm
Virtue of non-contention
Master this and you can say
I very humbly follow the Way

*Virtue of non-contention is remaining calm
by mastering this you come to no harm, be
able to say, I very humbly follow the Way*

Verse Sixty Nine

Play the host by being the guest
Not to advance but retreat instead
Shall move you forward
Without need for a road
Make friends of perceived enemies
Hold fast to your treasures
And do not lose
Sight of the qualities
You hold so dear
For in doing so will only cause dread
For the one who holds fast to these qualities
Shall always be
In control of their own faculty

No enemy shall you see by holding fast to compassion, frugality and humility

Verse Seventy

You do not have to know the Tao
To be living the Tao
My words simple, yet profound
So easy to be
Practicing the Tao just like me
To remain humble
Is a virtue still
The rest shall follow
And you can be
A beacon of light for others to see
A treasure doesn't have to be
Clad in gold for all to see
It can and is, contained in thee

A treasure doesn't have to be clad in gold for all to see, it can and is, contained in thee

Verse Seventy One

You don't know what you don't know
To think you know when you don't
Only leads to difficulty
Be open to learn
For then you grow
Be open to
What you don't know

*Being open to what you don't know,
leads the way for you to grow*

Verse Seventy Two

Approach each day
And hold in awe
Be open to all that is
For beauty and joy
Reside in here
Of this you shall never tire
So know thyself
And love thyself
And like the Sage
Remain humble
And in gratitude

Love yourself without ego, know yourself without attitude and like the Sage, always remain in gratitude

Verse Seventy Three

To be humble and meek
Says more than you think
With this you can lead the way
To be fearless in being timid
Is to key to staying alive
To be fearless in being bold
Can only cause you harm
For Heaven excels in overcoming
Yet it does not contend
Responds but does not speak
Attracts but does not summon
In laying plans yet seems slack
It is because it does not command
That we continue to follow

To be humble and meek, says more than you think,
be fearless in being strong and in doing no wrong

Verse Seventy Four

Death is but a stage of life
Not to be feared but purely revered
For as surely as we are born
We eventually die
We leave our earthly body behind
To have no fear in death
Is to achieve your dreams
For more is accomplished
If surrender to all is attained
It is for this reason
Do no harm to your fellow man
As the Lord of Death
Shall take care of the rest

We are born, we leave, cause no harm to your fellow man, as the Lord of Death takes care of the rest

Verse Seventy Five

If the people are hungry
Surely the taxes are too high
If the people are difficult
Surely those in authority are too
To lead by example
Works both ways
To gain peace and harmony
Those in authority first set the example
For what the people see they follow
Don't overtax yourself on any level
Lead those around you by how
you would like to be led
Value for what you have
Is more important
Than value for what you don't have

Life is calmer when we don't want for more, lead as you wish to be led, for there is much to be gained from a positive attitude and always living in gratitude

Verse Seventy Six

Man who is supple
Shall surely live long
Trees which are pliant and fragile when alive
Like man are dried and shrivelled when dead
Thus the supple and weak
The hard and the strong
Are both
Sides of life and death
To be supple and weak
To be flexible
Is better than being
Dry and brittle
And broken

The hard and the stiff can be broken, to be supple and flexible is to prevail especially amid the storm

Verse Seventy Seven

The way of heaven is to take from
What is in excess to make
Good what is deficient
The way of man
Is that of reverse
Follow the Way
Is to follow the lead
Set by Heaven
As the way to succeed
Let go of greed
And give what you can
This benefits all, not just your
Fellow man

*Let go of greed and share if you can, let
benefits flow to your fellow man*

Verse Seventy Eight

There is nothing more submissive and weak than water
Yet for attacking that which is hard and strong
Nothing can surpass it
There is nothing that can take its place
The weak overcome the strong
The submissive overcome the hard
Yet no one can put this information into practice
One who takes on humility
Is worthy of being a ruler
One who takes on the understanding of himself
Is one who follows the Way
Can surely say
More is accomplished
By being meek
It has greater rewards than you may think

Understanding yourself is to understand you fellow man, to be humble and meek is to be like water, it gently erodes that which is unyielding, have a soft approach to all that you do, this also means be gentle with you

Verse Seventy Nine

Once trust is broken
Yet friendship regained
There still remains
Unspoken ground
There are those who give
There are those who get
There are some things
We wish to forget
Yet do we wish to live with regret?
If not, then its best
We do forgive and do forget

*To follow the Way is to forgive and forget,
lest we end up living with deep regret*

Verse Eighty

To follow the Way
Is to be content
Happiness is found within oneself
Happiness is not found 'outside'
Happiness is knowing the Tao
Happiness is having weapons but no need to use them
Happiness is using your hands to create
Happiness is living in peace
Happiness is being at one with your neighbour
Keeping things simple and uncomplicated

*Keep it simple, keep it calm, appreciate all
you have and do no harm, a simple recipe for
you to live, in alignment with all that is*

Verse Eighty One

Understand the Tao
Needs no learning
Words are meaningless
If not sincere
Possessions are meaningless
If you do not share
Those who share are richer
Those who know the Tao
Richer still
To understand your true essence
The gift with which you came
Is the true measure
We come with nothing
We leave with nothing
Use it wisely

We come with nothing, we leave with nothing, understanding is all there is

POSTSCRIPT

I hope and trust you have gained something from reading the 81 Verses of the Tao Te Ching. They are not complex, they are a simple, yet profound blueprint as a way of going about our daily life.

The words suggest we should look inside ourselves, our behaviours and how we treat others. It is not about 'others' it is about 'us', our motives, our dreams, how to be the best possible version of ourselves and being open to what we don't know.

It is about speaking up and not harbouring resentment, about remaining calm, being fair not harsh, treating all with equality and not deploying deceit nor abuse of power.

The Tao states "if you take of the land you must give of the land", meaning: when you clear land to build a house (for example) you must then plant trees and shrubs for the birds and the bees, restore the natural order. Do not take…without giving. The Earth cannot sustain the constant 'taking' which is occurring at an alarming rate, we must give something back. It is a RESPECTful way to live and be.

Since writing and completing these verses I take a moment each morning to read some of them, I find it leaves me with a calm and appreciative attitude… and … reminds me to be a nice person for the day!

I hope too, you will see the value of these words and be able to integrate them into your life and do so by being 'present' to your actions, words and deeds.

Always remember to be: *an individual, just like me…*

Much love

About the Author

I was born in Tasmania, Australia in the picturesque Huon Valley, the youngest of three children.

Writing was not on my radar until my son died in tragic circumstances when he took his own life whilst in Risdon Prison. He had a severe mental illness and was only receiving minimal medication; it would be sufficient to bring any parent to the brink. I survived thanks to the Holistic Wheel Theory…a theory of which I was blissfully unaware.

In my first book 'I MAKE MARK' I outline the Holistic Wheel Theory and my life from 1952-2000, ending subsequent to the death of my son in custody. Hopefully 'READ HEED LEAD' will further explain the Holistic Wheel Theory, as channelled by Lao Tze and how it relates to what I titled 'My Recipe for Dealing with Life's Challenges.

In my life 'fact is stranger than fiction', and this becomes evident as I journey thru time recounting my life. BEYOND DESCRIPTION a story of grief, disbelief and insight… (the second book in the story of my life) will detail how and when the revered Lao Tze entered my life and how my life was forever changed.

I am spiritual and believe in the power of positivity.

In 2009 I fully opened to channel Spirit and with it came a whole new realm of possibility, one which enriched my life but also left me feeling isolated and alone on planet Earth.

My education is mostly and more importantly gained from the 'University of Life' where I learned that we are given challenges for a reason, they are not a form of punishment …merely challenges which assist us to learn, grow and evolve…which after all…is the reason we come to Earth.

At 67 I am still learning and shall continue to do so; I encourage you to continue on your individual path and become the very best version of yourself you can possibly be. Regardless of age…you can still achieve that which is important to you. Much love.

Acknowledgement

Acknowledgement and well deserved thanks to:

Julie-Ann Harper and her team at the Pickawoowoo Publishing Group.

This book would not have been possible without the invaluable assistance of these wonderful humans.

The vision I have is one aspect, turning that vision into a reality is a true work of art and professionalism, so to the Pickawoowoo Publishing team, I am truly grateful and very appreciative.

Much love and thanks

www.ingramcontent.com/pod-product-compliance
Lightning Source LLC
Chambersburg PA
CBHW072100290426
44110CB00014B/1754